American Quilter's Society

2007

CATALOGUE of

SHOW QUILTS

Semi-finalists in the 23rd Annual

Quilt Show & Contest
PADUCAH, KENTUCKY

Located in Paducah, Kentucky, the American Quilter's Society (AQS) is dedicated to promoting the accomplishments of today's quilters. Through its publications and events, AQS strives to honor today's quiltmakers and their work and to inspire future creativity and innovation in quiltmaking.

Editor: Bonnie K. Browning
Graphic Design: Elaine Wilson
Cover Design: Michael Buckingham
Photography: Supplied by the individual quiltmakers

Additional copies of this book may be ordered from the American Quilter's Society, PO Box 3290, Paducah, KY 42002-3290; 800-626-5420 (orders only please); or online at www.AmericanQuilter.com. For all other inquiries, call 270-898-7903.

Proudly printed and bound in the United States of America

Each year the quilts entered in the AQS Quilt Contest show us the best of traditional techniques, and how they push the envelope with the very latest innovative trends. It is a pleasure to present the semi-finalists in the 23rd Annual AQS Quilt Show.

The quilts range from bed-sized to miniatures. Quilts made as wall art explore techniques like photo imagery, stenciling, painting, and threadwork. The new Young Designers category challenges younger quilters, from 18 to 35, to make a quilt using any technique in an innovative way. Computerized embroidery and quilting have taken artistry into a whole new realm of design possibilities.

Quilters from 47 U.S. States and 14 countries entered this year's contest.

Make your plans now to enter the 2008 AQS Quilt Contest.

Meredith Schroeder

Meredith Schroeder
AQS President and Founder

101, ROSES FOR MATTIE, 82" x 82"
Irma Gail Hatcher, Conway, AR

102, ORGANIC GARDEN, 86½" x 86½"
Bonnie Keller, Chehalis, WA

103, VICTORIAN ROSETTE, 81" x 81"
Jean Lohmar, Galesburg, IL

**104, DEEP IN THE HEART OF TEXAS,
MY CHILDHOOD HOME IN GRAPEVINE**
74" x 88", Suzanne Louth, Springfield, MO

Inspired by tiles by William Frend De Morgan, (1839-1917)

105, AND DRAGONS, TOO…, 73½" x 92"
Suzanne Marshall, Clayton, MO

106, FLOW BLUE, 78" x 87"
Kathy Munkelwitz & Nancy Sammis, Isle, MN

107, THE BONAVENTURE YEARS, 93" x 94"
Jennifer Patriarche & Wanda Rains, Bellevue, WA

108, JOURNEY HAND IN HAND, 94" x 94"
Lahala Phelps, Bonney Lake, WA

Samuel Williams Album Quilt, ©The Baltimore Museum of Art

Patterns by Pat Andreatta

Botanical Wreaths by Laura Reinstatler: That Patchwork Place

109, BUTTERFLIES & ROSES, 108" x 108"
Marsha D. Radtke, Crossville, TN

110, BOTANICAL WREATHS, 107" x 107"
Jerre Reese, Murrells Inlet, SC

111, FLOWER OF LIFE, 87" x 87"
Sharon Schamber, Payson, AZ

112, GRACE UNFOLDING, 80¼" x 80½"
Betty Ekern Suiter, Racine, WI

113, SHADE OF PICAKE, 83" x 83"
Takako Takada, Yokohama, Kanagawa, Japan

114, SYMPHONY OF TWIGS, 81" x 81"
Fusako Takido, Shizuoka City, Shizuoka, Japan

115, METHODIST MEMORIES, 85" x 95"
Kathryn Tennyson, Chestertown, NY

201, AUTUMN FLOWER PARK, 83" x 95"
Kimi Aoki, Chikuma, Nagano, Japan

Inspired by an old calendar, author unknown

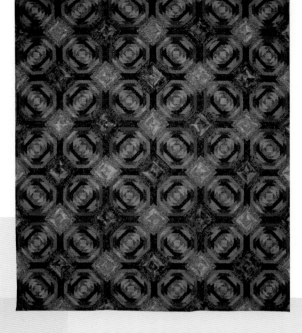

Pheasant, Sasser by Liz Schwartz, *Quilts with Style* #42, August 2003

202, A SNAIL OF A TRAIL, 74" x 89"
Donna Brannen, Macon, GA

203, SHAWNEE FOREST, 81" x 95"
Janet Coen, Golconda, IL

204, FOLLOW ME, 84" x 84"
Margaret Curley, Pittsburgh, PA

205, EVERLASTING WREATH… OF LOVE, 104" x 94"
Dawn Eckrich, Iowa City, IA

Mariner's Compass Quilts New Directions by Judy Mathieson, C & T Publishing, Inc.

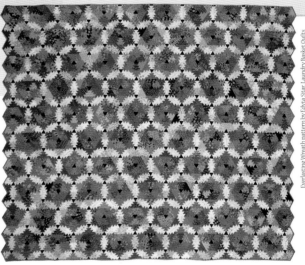

Everlasting Wreath pattern by Edyta Sitar, Laundry Basket Quilts

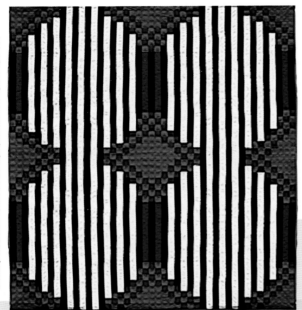

Southwest by Southwest: Native American and Mexican Designs by Kirsten Olsen. Sterling Publishing Company

Patchwork Portfolio: A Presentation of 165 Original Quilt Designs by Jinny Beyer. Howell Press Inc.

206, NAVAJO CHIEF (WITH 4 QUILTED THUNDERBIRDS),
88" x 101", Mary E. Glassmeyer, Tualatin, OR

207, NEPTUNE'S MOTHER-IN-LAW, 80" x 80"
Gwenfai Rees Griffiths, Abergele, North Wales, UK

208, EDA'S LILIES, 82" x 102"
Tone Haugen-Cogburn, Maryville, TN

209, CACOPHONOUS PROGRESSION, 82" x 98½"
Barbara Jahn, Medellin, Antioquia, Colombia, SA

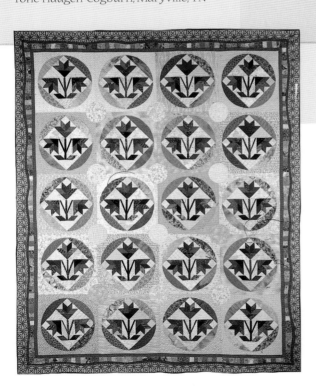

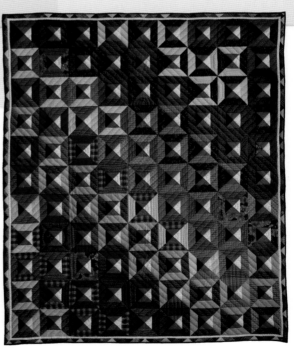

Glorious Patchwork by Kaffe Fasset, Clarkson N. Potter Publishers

Treasury of American Quilts: Including Complete Patterns and Instructions for Making Your Own Quilts by Cyril I. Nelson & Carter Houck. Crown Publishers; Feathers That Fly by Lee Cleland, Martingale & Co, Inc.

210, BASKET CASE, 92½" x 110"
Cookie Litttle, Cape Girardeau, MO

211, ALMOST AMISH, 81" x 81"
Jean Lohmar, Galesburg, IL

212, MY FAVORITE COLORS, 87" x 96"
Ann Crowl Meyer, Richland Center, WI

213, RAINBOW STARS – AN EXPERIMENT IN COLOR
87" x 104", Diane A. Myers, Pueblo West, CO

Quiltmaking by Hand: Simple Stitches, Exquisite Quilts by Jinny Beyer, Breckling Press

I'll Sing You Seven O, Green Grow the Rushes O! by Ann Fettelson, Quilter's Newsletter Magazine, April 2004 Cover

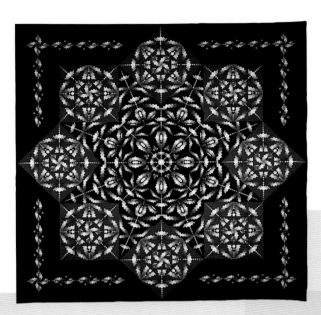

Granny Quilts by Darlene Zimmerman, Krause Publications; workshop with Darlene Zimmerman

214, LOG CABIN / KALEIDOSCOPE, 84" x 84"
Fumiko Ohkawa, Kobe, Hyogo, Japan

215, '30'S FLOWER BASKET, 82½" x 96"
Linda Rasmussen, Monrovia, CA

216, VIVÉ A LA ORANGE, 100" x 106"
Roberta Reskusich, Glen Carbon, IL

217, STARS IN MY HAND, 98" x 98"
Nadine Ruggles, Gerlingen, Germany

New York Beauty pattern by Karen K. Stone, Electric Quilt Company

Stars Classic American Quilt Collection by Janet Wickell and Darra Duffy Williamson, Rodale Press

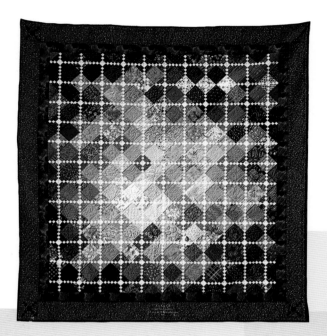

Sleeping Beauty pattern by Susan Garman, Quakertown Quilts

218, CRISS CROSS QUILT, 91" x 92"
Emmy Schmidt, Evansville, IN

219, SCARLET BEAUTY, 82" x 99½"
Kathryn Sims, Alexis, IL

220, BEWITCHED, BOTHERED & BEWILDERED
93" x 93", V. Wayne Sneath, Northfield, IL

221, CELESTIAL SHOWERS, 86" x 86"
Mildred Sorrells, Macomb, IL

Nearly Insane by Liz Lois, Liz & Lois Publications

222, SON COMPASS, 86" x 86"
Elizabeth Spannring, La Center, WA

223, NOVEMBER FIELDS, 89" x 89"
Gail Stepanek, New Lenox, IL

224, BURGOYNE REVISITED, 80" x 97"
Carole Sutton, Lowell, IN

225, ROMANCE ROSE, 86" x 100"
Teresa Varnes, Vista, CA

Nancy J Martin's 365 Quilt Blocks Perpetual Calendar, That Patchwork Place; Rose: Rose Bur by Ernest B Haight, hand quilted by Isabel Haight. Quilter's Newsletter Magazine, #191, April 1987

Feathered Star Quilt Blocks I by Marsha McCloskey Feathered Star Productions, Inc.

226, RED FEATHERED STARS, 86" x 86"
Pauline Warren, Sidney, OH

227, WITHOUT / WITHIN, 65" x 87"
Kent Williams & Nancy Fisher, Madison, WI

228, ABOVE PARADISE, 87" x 88"
Louise Young, Tioga, PA

301, JACK'S CHAIN, 86" x 95"
Sharon K. Bowman, Fort Worth, TX

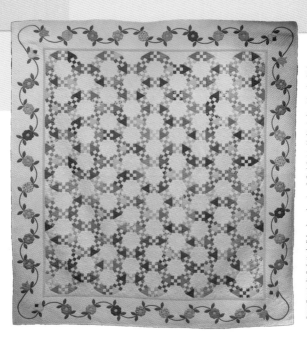
Scraps Organized to Perfection by DeLoa Jones, American Quilter's Society. Machine Appliqué: A Sampler of Techniques by Sue Nickels, American Quilter's Society.

Woman's Day Book of American Needlework, Rose Wilder Lane, 1963

302, PRINCE'S FEATHERS: RISING SUN, 83" x 83"
Mary Chalmers, Willmar, MN

303, PATCHES OF RAINBOW, 89" x 89"
Barbara Clem, Rockford, IL

304, THE ANCIENT MARINER AT SUNRISE
83¼" x 84½", Patricia L. Delaney, Abington, MA

305, THROUGH THE WOODS TO GRANDMA'S HOUSE, 82" x 94"
Cindy Vermillion Hamilton, Pagosa Springs, CO

Husqvarna Viking Embroidery Disks #1 & #5

Ozark Varieties by Kathy Kansier

306, SPIDER, SPIDER WHERE ART THOU…
80½" x 80½", Valeta Hensley, Flemington, MO

307, FLORAL ARRANGEMENT, 88" x 88"
Ann Horton, Redwood Valley, CA

308, PALMETTE, 84" x 84"
Atsuko Kuwada, Kawasaki, Kanagawa, Japan

309, NEBRASKA'S RISING SUN, 84½" x 85"
Sandra J. McMillan, Albion, NE

Rose Sampler Supreme by Rosemary Makhan, Martingale & Company/That Patchwork Place

310, WALL FLOWER, 84" x 84"
Philippa Naylor, Beverly, East Yorkshire, UK

311, ROSE GARDEN SAMPLER, 85½" x 100¼"
Patricia Pfeifle, Parrish, FL

312, SPIN DANCER, 98" x 98"
Sharon Schamber, Payson, AZ

313, MILLE FLEURS, 77" x 89"
Valli Schiller, Naperville, IL

314, CONESTOGA COVERUP, 87½" x 87½"
Shirley Stutz, Lore City, OH

315, IRISH ROSE, 100" x 100"
Nancy A. Swisher, Fairmont, WV

316, AUTOMNE · PRINTEMPS, 76" x 85½"
Yoko Takahashi, Adachi, Tokyo, Japan

317, FALKLAND – A COVENTRY CHINTZ MEDALLION
98" x 101", Mary Abbott Williams, Pinehurst, NC

Appliqué Masterpiece Little Brown Bird Patterns by Margaret Docherty, American Quilter's Society; workshop with Yoko Saito

Rosebud Embroidery Designs by Jenny Haskins, Quilter's Resource, Inc.

Panache by Dinah Jeffries, Garden City Gateworks

Applique 12 Borders and Medallions by Elly Sienkiewicz, C & T Publishing, Inc.; Nature's Chorus and Forget Me Knots by Jeana Kimball; Foxglove Cottage Red and Green Folk Art Quilt Pattern by Jennifer Buechel; www.ornamentalapplique.com; Jacobean Rhapsodies: Composing With 28 Applique Designs by Patricia Campbell & Mimi Ayars; C & T Publishing, Inc.; The Best Of Jacobean Applique Includes Exotica And Romantica Patterns by Patricia Campbell & Mimi Ayars; American Quilters Society; Lady Birds Rose Garden pattern by Darlene Christopherisen; Floral Applique by Nancy Pearson; EZ Quilting by Wrights; Fleurs du Jardin by Lisa DeBee Schiller; Love Birds wallhanging by Suzanne Marshall

401, BED OF ROSES, 85½" x 86"
Esther Aliu, Donvale, Victoria, Australia

402, HOUSTON COUNTY ELEGANCE, 82½" x 82½"
Michele Barnes, Grapeland, TX

403, THE PEONY QUILT, 70" x 85"
Karen Barr, Springfield, IL

404, THE COMET, 83" x 102"
Jan Beckert, Newfane, VT

Vermont Quilt Festival Collection Hoopla Patterns

Rose Marie's Lace by Helen Squire, American Quilter; Spring 2006

Star of Bethlehem, Laura Nownes, The Quilt Digest Press

Summer Romance by Glad Creations

405, FLORAL STAR OF 2006, 86½" x 87¼"
Belinda Betts, Orange, NSW, Australia,

406, SUMMER WEDDING, 84" x 106"
Karen Blocher, Unionville, IN

407, FLOWER POWER, 77" x 88"
Lynn Droege, Overland Park, KS

408, DAZZLING STAR, 90½" x 90¼"
Elaine Dyson, Ulverstone, Tasmania, Australia

Cinco de Mayo by Karen K. Stone, The Electric Quilt Company

Baltimore Beauties and Beyond Studies in Classic Album Quilt Appliqué Vol.1 and Baltimore Album Quilts: Historic Notes and Antique Patterns Patterns Companion to Baltimore Beauties and Beyond, and Dimensional Appliqué Baskets, Blooms, and Baltimore Borders by Elly Sienkiewicz, C & T Publishing, Inc. and Spoken Without a Word by Elly Sienkiewicz, The Turtle Hill Press

409, TIDINGS OF JOY, 106" x 106"
Mae Garrett Elliott, Colorado Springs, CO

410, PEARLS FROM GRANDMA, 88" x 88"
Tammy Finkler, Conklin, MI

411, MY BALTIMORE, 77" x 95"
Janet K. Gunn, Rapid City, SD

412, FOR THE LOVE OF HAND QUILTING, 96" x 97"
Carole Hirsch, Evansville, IN

The Best of Baltimore Beauties, The Best of Baltimore Beauties (Part II), and Baltimore Beauties and Beyond by Elly Sienkiewicz, C & T Publishing, Inc.

Original design by Sue Schmieden, The Quilting Connection, Elkhorn, WI

Infinite Feathers Quilting Designs by Anita Shackelford, American Quilters Society. Think Small by Shirley Thompson, Powell Publications/Golden Threads; Birds Color by Number Western Publishing Co., Inc.; reproduction of appliqué quilt top by Susanna Culp, 1948, Gettysburg, PA

413, OH, SUSANNA, 85½" x 96½"
Laurie Johnson, Brookfield, WI

414, KULA GARDEN, 96" x 96"
Satoko Kato, Kamakura, Kanagawa, Japan

415, LAVENDER BLUE, 89" x 89"
Judith A. Laurini, Churchville, NY

416, ROMER AND LEN'S DOUBLE WEDDING RING,
78" x 91", Kathy Englert Lee, West Linn, OR

Jacobean Appliqué Book I: Exotica and Book II: Romantica by Patricia Campbell & Mimi Ayers, American Quilter's Society

John Flynn's Double Wedding Ring Step by Step; Flynn Quilt Frame Co.

417, FOR MY SON, 74" x 81"
Kum Sook Lee, Yeonsu, Incheon, South Korea

418, THE BLACK RINGS, 64" x 80"
Susan Leise, Cedar Rapids, NE

419, TUSCAN PLAZA, 108" x 108"
Cheryl Malkowski, Roseburg, OR

420, MONSTERA, 109" x 109"
Molly Miles, McKinleyville, CA

421, BLUE MEDALLION, 83¾" x 90"
Eunice Palffy-Muhoray, Kent, OH

422, HUMMINGBIRD HEAVEN, 88½" x 110"
Mary E. Piper, Racine, WI

423, FROM THE SOUTH OF FRANCE, 84" x 84"
Patricia Probst, Columbus, IN

424, BUCK AND THE DEERE, 70" x 90"
Mary C.. Randolph, Chelsea, MI

On the Farm pattern by Claire Oehler, The Country Quilter. *Times and Seasons: A Piecemakers Calendar and Quilt Book,* Piecemakers, Costa Mesa, CA, 2003

425, CELESTIAL GARDEN – NO DOGS ALLOWED, 84" x 84", Eleanor Schultz, Anderson, SC

426, TRAVELER'S TREE, 84" x 84", Mutsuko Shindo, Kaigan, Fujisawa, Japan

427, STRAWBERRY FANTASY, 74" x 85", Mie Totsu, Nagano City, Nagano, Japan

428, EMMA'S COURTYARD, 90" x 90", Dee Van Driel, Fitchburg, WI

Emma's Courtyard by Jo Morton, Jo Morton Quilts, Nebraska City, NE

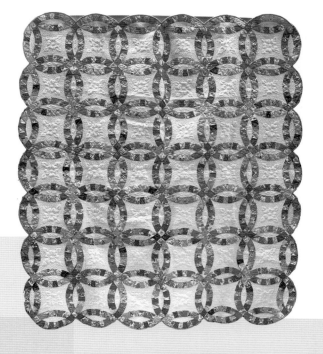

429, BITTERSWEET, 89" x 89"
Jane Zillmer, Mercer, WI

430, LOVE AMONGST THE BRIARS, 90½" x 106"
Bronwyn van 't Hof, Beaumaris, VIC, Australia

501, BLANDFORD'S ALBUM, 104" x 104"
The Blandford Quilters, Venice, FL

502, GALVESTON BAY BLUES, 100" x 107"
Island Quilter's Guild, Galveston, TX

503, VINTAGE GARDEN, 83¾" x 83¾"
Terri Krysan, Lakeville, MN

504, NAALC 2006 COLUMBIA AUCTION QUILT,
96" x 96", Ladies of the Knights and Knights of the
Needle, Winston-Salem, NC

505, CENTENNIAL QUILT, 102" x 116½"
Marie Johansen & Rainshadow Quilting Arts Guild,
Friday Harbor, WA

**506, ROSES ROUGES MYSTIQUES
(MYSTIC RED ROSES),** 86" x 86", Myri Lehman
Tapungot, Cagayan de Oro, Mindanao, Philippines

507, NAVIGATING THE STARS, 96" x 96"
Mary K. Ryan, Jan Snelling McTaggart, and
Vermont Quilt Festival, Rutland, VT

509, FLORAL FANTASY, 90" x 112"
West Pasco Quilters Guild, Inc., Hudson, FL

508, FINDING UNITY, 74" x 93½"
Jan Wass, Kathy Drew, &
Village Quilters of Loudon, TN

601, BALTIMORE ALBUM QUILT, 74" x 88½"
Haeok Chang, Seongnam, Gyeonggi, South Korea

Patterns by Dianne Johnston, Dianne Johnston Products, Australia

Samuel Williams Album Quilt. ©The Baltimore Museum of Art

602, A MYTHIC WORLD, 80" x 80"
Mi Sun Chang, Seoul, South Korea

603, TRIBUTE TO FELIX, 71½" x 89"
Fleda Collins, Talbott, TX

604, REFLECTIONS IN THE MOONLIGHT,
82½" x 82½", Sherry K. Durbin, Burnsville, NC

605, BLACK ANTIQUE SUNBURSTS, 82" x 96"
Linda Dyken, Mobile, AL

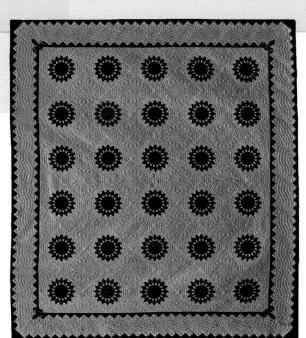

606, FAIRY DUST, 87½" x 87½"
Kelora Lee Goethe, Knoxville, TN

607, BLESSING, 85" x 85"
Ikuko Hagino, Yokohama, Kanagawa, Japan

608, THE SEA OF ONE'S BIRTH PLACE, 80" x 86"
Tsueko Kamataki, Inage, Chiba, Japan

609, CHEERS! 82" x 82"
Shizuyo Morishita, Ota, Tokyo, Japan

610, FOREVER, 82" x 82"
Felisa Nakazawa, Ueda, Nagano, Japan

611, FLOWER WINDOW, 80" x 80"
Ichiko Ogura, Tokyo, Japan

612, BIRDS IN PARADISE, 90" x 90"
Karolyn Reker, Cartersville, GA

613, I MUST BE HEXED, 90¼" x 115"
Cheryl L. See, Ashburn, VA

614, IN FULL SPLENDOR, 80" x 80"
Akemi Sugiyama, Hamura, Tokyo, Japan

615, GARDEN OF HEAVEN, 60" x 81"
Noriko Tagata, Suruga, Shizuoka City, Japan

701, CIRCLES X, 72" x 51"
Mary Jo Bowers, Chicago, IL

702, GARDEN, 83" x 67"
Beth Brady, Marietta, GA

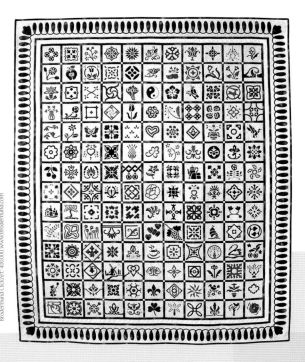

Dutch Treat: 196 Applique Blocks Inspired by Delft Designs by Judy Garden, Martingale & Company/That Patchwork Place. Broderbund ClickArt® 400,000. www.broderbund.com

Artful Album Quilts by Jane Townswick, Martingale & Company/That Patchwork Place

703, LA BELLE ROUGE, 64" x 79"
Mary Chester, Rantoul, IL

704, SUDDENLY IT WAS LAVENDER, 81¼" x 98½"
Jane Cullyford, Calhan, CO

**705, CHARMING CHAMOMILE &
THE SUGAR CUBES,** 64" x 43½"
Mickey Depre, Oak Lawn, IL

706, MAILE LEAF LEI, 75" x 75"
Karen Esterholdt, Portland, OR

Patterns by Jean Brown, Jeans Impressions; Mary Haunani Cesar, Mary's Treasures; Elizabeth Root, Elizabeth Root Designs Hawaii, Inc., and Pacific Rim Quilt Company

Flower Fairy Patterns by Reva Roark Stewart

Baltimore Album Quilts, A Pattern Companion to Baltimore Beauties and Beyond; The Best of Baltimore Beauties, Part I, Papercuts and Plenty, Vol. III of Baltimore Beauties and Beyond; Applique 12 Borders & Medallions; Patterns from Easy to Heirloom by Elly Sienkiewicz, C & T Publishing, Spoken Without a Word by Elly Sienkiewicz, The Turtle Hill Press

707, WILD FLOWERBELLES, 68" x 72"
Nancy Gilliland, Somers, MT

708, A THING OF BEAUTY IS A JOY FOREVER, KEATS, 77" x 77", Atsuko Griffin, Pueblo, CO

709, MEMORY OF 60TH BIRTHDAY, 65" x 73"
Saeko Hasumuro, Okayama City, Okayama, Japan

710, PARADISE, 72" x 86"
Hatsune Hirano, Honjo, Saitama, Japan

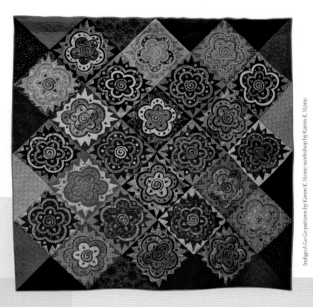

Indigo A Go Go pattern by Karen K. Stone; workshop by Karen K. Stone

711, FIREWHEELS, 79" x 50"
Judy Kriehn, Garland, TX

712, TREASURED INSANITY, 75" x 75"
Laura Markus, Gemantown, MD

713, HAWAIIAN-BALTIMORE MISSION, 66" x 66"
Linda Postlethwait, Anchorage, AK

714, THE WEDDING, 86" x 86"
Shirley Pound, Quitman, AR

Applique with Folded Cutwork by Anita Shackelford American Quilter's Society; Papercuts and Plenty Vol III of Baltimore Beauties and Beyond by Elly Sienkiewicz, C & T Publishing, Inc.

Affairs of the Heart, Applique Masterpiece by Ave Rossmann, American Quilter's Society

Jacobean Applique Book II: Romantica by Patricia Campbell & Mimi Ayers, American Quilter's Society

715, TACHYCARDIA, 75½" x 75"
Barbara K. Powers, Centreville, VA

716, THURSDAY AFTERNOON, 83½" x 69½"
Karol Saxberg, Sutherlin, OR

717, TWILIGHT FRIENDS, 62" x 66"
Judy Sheridan, Skaneateles Falls, NY

718, FIESTA DE TALAVERA, 72" x 72"
J. Michelle Watts & Rita Galaska, Roswell, NM

801, NUMBER TWO, 76" x 75"
Esther Aliu, Donvale, Victoria, Australia

802, REST OF A FOREST
60" x 62", Mieko Arai,
Izumizaki-Nisisirakawa, Fukushima, Japan

803, THE RISING SUN, 81" x 90"
Chiemi Asaka, Mitaka, Tokyo, Japan

804, POPPY BASKETS, 84½" x 84½"
Marlies Brandt, Wintersville, OH

Feathered Star pattern, *Easy Big Blocks* by Cindi Edgerton, McCalls Pattern Company

805, OH MY STARS, 72½" x 72½"
Anna Fell, Georgetown, TX

806, COLOR DANCE, 90" x 90"
Bette Haddon, DeFuniak Springs, FL

807, SOUTHERN OREGON HIGHLIGHTS, 64¾" x 59"
Karen Hanken, Jacksonville, OR

808, LOOSE CURVES, 64" x 64"
Dianne S. Hire, Northport, ME

809, ENTICEMENT, 62½" x 73¾"
Klonda Holt, Lee's Summit, MO

810, CINNAMON STAR, 72" x 72"
Julie Yaeger Lambert, Erlanger, KY

811, CRÈME BRULEE, 106" x 106"
Cheryl Malkowski, Roseburg, OR

812, CINCO DE MAYO, 72" x 72"
Christine Martinson & Monica Troy, Plainfield, IL

Op-Art Quilt Illusions Fast, Fun & Fabulous 3-D Illusions by Marilyn Doheny, Doheny Publications Inc.

813, IMAGE OF SPRING, 68" x 68"
Heejoung Oh, Moorpark, CA

814, EXCHANGE, 85" x 85"
Yeon Hee Park, Seongnam, Gyeonggi
South Korea

815, FINE FEATHERED FANCY, 81" x 81"
Ann L. Petersen, Aurora, CO

816, SPINNING OUT SPINNING IN 1, 70" x 57"
Helen Remick, Seattle, WA

Classic English Medallion Style Quilts by Bettina Havig, American Quilter's Society, quilting designs by Helen Squire, Karen McTavish, and Bobbie Smith

817, KALEIDOSCOPE TWIST, 73" x 74"
Birgit Schueller, Riegelsberg, Germany

818, NOT QUITE OLD WORLD, 70½" x 70"
Bobbie Smith, Avondale, AZ

819, GLORY, 62" x 62"
Etsuko Uto, Kashima City, Ibaraki, Japan

820, SOLID CHAOS, 61" x 40½"
Eileen Vince, Livonia, MI

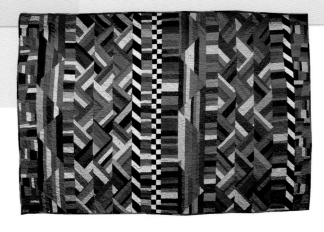

821, DEFINITELY FLOORED, 72½" x 73"
Ann Visman, Orange, NSW, Australia

822, HEARTSONG, 74¼" x 73½"
Elsie Vredenburg, Tustin, MI

823, BUCKSKIN, 78" x 79"
Marla Yeager, Ava, MO

901, TIED IN KNOTS, 68" x 45"
Sylvain Bergeron, Oswego, IL

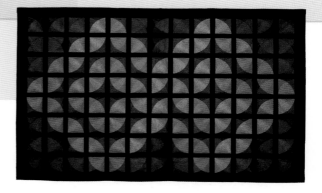

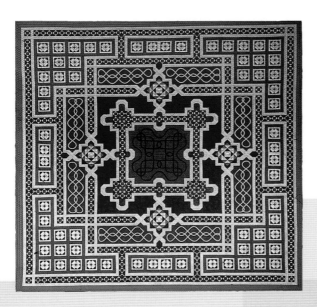

902, OSGOODE HALL, 68" x 68"
Jean Biddick & Jo Cady-Bull, Tucson, AZ

903, NAUTILUS MANDALA, 78" x 78"
Amy Bright, Tucson, AZ

904, YOUNG AT HEART©, 87" x 85"
Mary S. Buvia, Greenwood, IN

905, HOW DELIGHTFUL OUR LOVE IS! 65" x 70"
Eun Ryoung Choi, Seocho, Seoul, South Korea

906, GLOWING SPLENDOR, 62" x 78"
Barbara Cline, Bridgewater, VA

907, 5¢ A RIDE, 91½" x 91"
Babe Dodson, Sun City, AZ

908, AGUA CALIENTE, 76" x 49"
Doria A. Goocher, San Diego, CA

909, ATMOSPHERIC CONDITION, 81" x 58"
Barbara Oliver Hartman, Flower Mound, TX

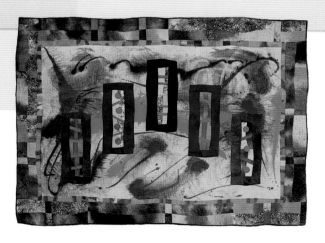

910, DRESDEN GALAXY, 79" x 79"
Mary Ann Herndon, The Woodlands, TX

911, ROMANCE, 68½" x 68½"
Akemi Hirasawa, Setagaya, Tokyo, Japan

912, HARVEST MOON WOOL QUILT, 69" x 89½"
Patricia A. Hobbs, Macomb, IL

913, THE QUILTED MANTLE, 78¼" x 100½"
Jaynette Huff, Conway, AR

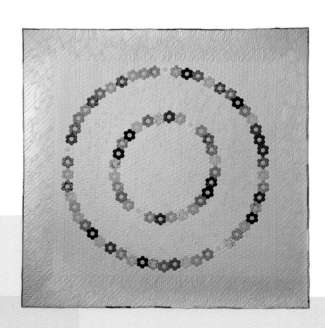

914, POEM OF MIDNIGHT, 60" x 60"
Hung-Sook Jang, Icheon, Kyunggi, South Korea

915, 10 YEARS AGO, 79" x 79"
Mikyung Jang, Seodaemoon, Seoul, South Korea

916, COUNTRY ROAD, 65" x 76"
Masumi Kako, Nagano City, Nagano, Japan

917, LUCKY THIRTEEN, 64½" x 64½"
Michael Kashey, Edinboro, PA

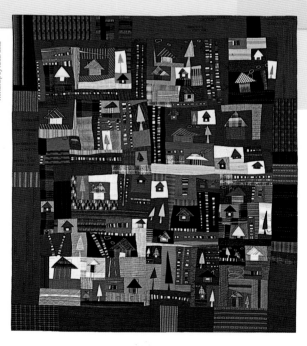

Workshop by Keiko Goke

Embracing Couple by Gustav Klimt (1898-99)

918, THE WINGS II, 67" x 68"
Mira Kim, Seongnam, Gyeonggi, South Korea

919, EMBRACING, 80" x 100"
Jung Sun Lee, Dongdaemun, Seoul, South Korea

920, A QUILTER'S SPACE FLIGHT, 66" x 82"
Elaine Letz, Copley, OH

921, THE HAPPY QUILT, 70" x 70"
Jeanne Lounsbury, Superior, CO

Piec'lique Curves the New Way by Sharon Schamber. American Quilter's Society. Mariner's Compass Quilts: New Directions by Judy Mathieson. C&T Publishing, Inc. Circle of Illusion pattern by Andrea Perejda.

922, AURUM, 60" x 64"
Joanne Mitchell, Geraldine, South Canterbury,
New Zealand

923, SUMMER FLOWERS, 66½" x 74"
Kathy Munkelwitz, Isle, MN

924, FLORADORA, 64½" x 76"
Claudia Clark Myers & Marilyn Badger, Duluth, MN

925, QUINTESSENTIAL QUAGMIRE QUILT
69½" x 56", Marie K. O'Kelley, Seattle, WA

926, A HAPPY TIME! 76" x 80"
Kayoko Oozono, Yokohama, Kanagawa, Japan

927, FLOWERS ALL A BLOOM'N, 90" x 110"
Maxine Renken, Blachly, OR

928, DREAM FLOWER III, 62" x 69"
Sachiko Sasakura, Tokyo, Japan

929, FANTASTIC FLOWERS, 77½" x 81""
Akiko Shiraishi, Narashino, Chiba, Japan

Bee Creative patterns by Nancy Davis Murry www.beecreativestudio.com

Diamond Wedding Ring pattern by Judy Niemeyer

930, PRAY, 86" x 86"
Masako Shoji, Sapporo, Hokkaido, Japan

931, BRIGHT FUTURE, 71" x 71"
Susan Diane Smith, Galiano Island,
British Columbia, Canada

932, LEAVES, 62" x 64"
Karen Spencer, Pella, IA

933, WILD THING, 69½" x 69½"
Rebecca Verrier-Watt, Harrisburg, NC

Photo of Lukas Rossi on drum by Jeff Bottari/Mark Burnett Productions; used with permission.

Jazz Attack Series patterns: Juke Box Quilts by Mona Baran & Carrie Strachan

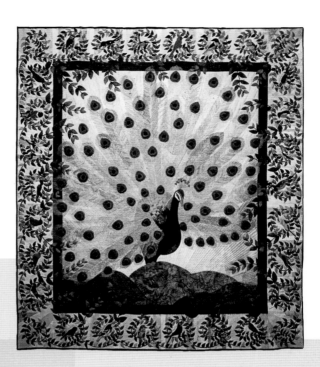

934, BULLSEYE! 62" x 72"
Cassandra Williams, Grants Pass, OR

935, BUT CAN HE SING? 76" x 80"
Roberta Williams, Milwaukee, WI

936, WINTER BLUE, 70" x 70"
Kyoko Yano, Sayama, Saitama, Japan

1001, THROUGH TUSCANY, 89" x 89"
Cynthia England, Dickinson, TX

1002, A QUIET PLACE, 62¼" x 47¼"
Lou Ann Estes, Oak Island, NC

1003, CAROUSEL CAPERS, 78" x 46½"
Shirley P. Kelly, Colden, NY

1004, RIVER OF LIFE, 66" x 66"
Inge Mardal & Steen Hougs, Chantilly, France

1005, GONE FISHIN, 64½" x 72"
Kathy McNeil, Tulalip, WA

1006, LIFE IN HOLLY RIDGE, 76" x 53"
Nancy Prince, Orlando, FL

1007, GRIZZLY BEAR, 83½" x 69"
Susanne M. Rasmussen, Simi Valley, CA

1008, FUNKADELIC, 67½" x 49½"
Shelli Ricci, Apple Valley, MN

1009, ON THE ROAD AGAIN, 73" x 52"
Linda S. Schmidt, Dublin, CA

1010, AMAZING SPRING IN THE ANTELOPE VALLEY
81" x 81, Rita Steffenson, Urbana, OH

1011, EVERGREEN, 62" x 68"
Carol Taylor, Pittsford, NY

1012, CLOWNS ON PARADE, 97" x 82"
Cathy Wiggins, Macon, NC

1013, IN LINE OF DUTY, 93" x 45"
Cassandra Williams, Grants Pass, OR

"The creative mind plays with the objects it loves."

Carl Jung

Baltimore Beauties & Beyond and Papercuts & Plenty Vol III of Baltimore Beauties & Beyond by Elly Sienkiewicz, C & T Publishing, Inc.

1101, SUMMER AFTERNOON, 56" x 56"
Connie Ayers, Belfair, WA

1103, ENDLESS SUMMER, 53" x 76"
Nancy S. Breland, Pennington, NJ

1104, PRAIRIE COMPASS – WORTH TWO COMPLEMENTS
56½" x 56½", Kathleen L. Carlson, Bridgeton, MO

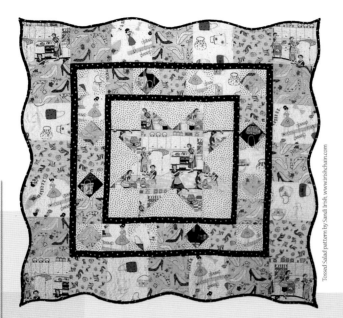

1105, HIDDEN TIKIS, 50" x 50"
Susan K. Cleveland, West Concord, MN

1106, MEMORIES OF MOM, 42½" x 42½"
Joanne Coughlin, Ann Arbor, MI

1107, COSMIC KALEIDOSCOPE, 40" x 40½"
Barbara Dowdy-Trabke, Reno, NV

1108, THISTLE, 56" x 56"
Sayoko Fujii, Shibuya, Tokyo, Japan

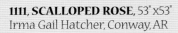

1109, COSMIC CUBE, 51" x 51"
Robin M. Haller, Carbondale, IL

1110, RED/PURPLE AGAIN, 53" x 72"
Lynne G. Harrill, Greenville, SC

1111, SCALLOPED ROSE, 53" x53"
Irma Gail Hatcher, Conway, AR

1112, GIRLIE GIRL, 56" x 56"
Wendy Hill, Sunriver, OR

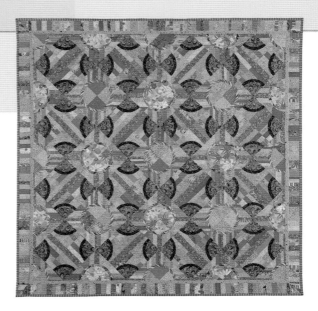

1113, CANDLELIGHT, 52" x 52"
Hatsune Hirano, Honjo, Saitama, Japan

1114, INDIGO PINES, 53" x 53"
Pat Holly, Muskegon, MI

1115, KRISTOPHER MAY'S QUILT, 56" x 54"
Klonda Holt, Lee's Summit, MO

1116, PURRRSONALITY, 54" x 60"
Sue Jones & Kathy Drew, Maryville, TN

Quilted Forest Decor and A Forest of Quilts by Terrie Kralik, Krause Publications; Log Cabin Scribbles and Stitches ...In the Sticks by Debbie Bryan & Rick Yancey (photographer), Blue Ridge Publications

Laurel Burch Fantastic Felines 47x60 Embroidery Collection CD, www.OESD.com

1117, ROMANCE, 57" x 57"
Julie Yaeger Lambert, Erlanger, KY

1118, VOYAGES, 44" x 78½"
Katherine Lincoln, Burke, VA

1119, JOY, 48½" x 49"
Rebecca Muir MacKellar, Canton, NY

1120, SOMERSAULTS, 46" x 54"
Janice Maddox, Asheville, NC

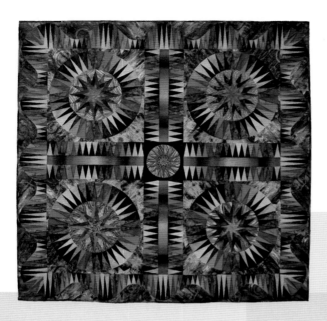

1121, RAINBOW REVOLUTION, 58½" x 58½"
Peggy Martin, San Diego, CA

1122, AMERICAN ROSE, 56" x 59½"
Irene Mueller, Kirkwood, MO

1123, A Study of Square Pattern, Part 2
57" x 57", Tadako Nagasawa, Nagoya, Japan

1124, LUMINIFEROUS, 44" x 44"
Susan Nelson, Prior Lake, MN

The Cactus Rose pattern by Judy Niemeyer

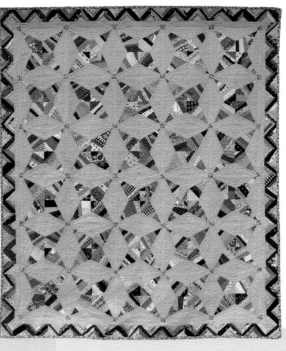

1125, STELLA FLORA: MARIA'S STORY
44" x 42", Kitty Niles, Sequim, WA

1126, SUGAR SACK STAR, 58" x 71"
Lorraine Olsen, Springfield, MO

1127, A TRIBUTE TO ISRAEL KAMAKAWIWOOLE
42" x 42", Bonnie Ouellette, Seneca, SC

1128, FANTASIA, 48" x 48"
Nancy Peters, Wildwood, MO

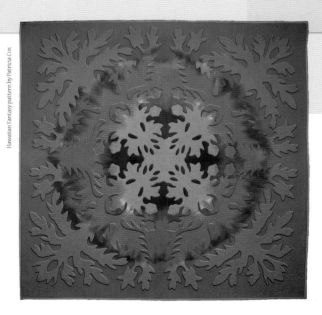

Hawaiian Fantasy pattern by Patricia Cox

Lone Star Quilts & Beyond Step-by-Step Projects and Inspiration by Jan Krentz, C & T Publishing, Inc.

1129, GRANDMA'S GAMEBOY, 41" x 41"
Sandra Peterson, Muncie, IN

1130, BIBBIDY BOP, 55" x 55"
Devin Ramsey, Carbondale, KS

1131, ROUND TRIP – SQUARED, 40" x 40"
Birgit Schueller, Riegelsberg, Germany

1132, SPLENDOR IN THE ROUND, 40" x 40"
Cindy Seitz-Krug, Bakersfield, CA

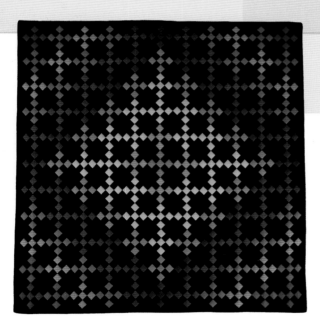

1133, GIFTS FROM GWEN, 58" x 58"
Joyce Stewart, Deweyville, UT

1134, RED HOT MAMA! 57" x 55"
Patricia L. Styring, St. Augustine, FL

1135, THE BIG BANG, 52¾" x 52¾"
Tess Thorsberg, Macon, GA

1136, ORANGE – RANGE, 52¼" x 52¼"'
Tomoko Toono, Ohta, Tokyo, Japan

1137, TEQUILA SUNSET, 47" x 47"
Monica Troy, Lemont, IL

1138, SUMMER RENTALS, 51½" x 58"'
Martha Walker, Phoenix, AZ

1139, ROGALAND ROSEMALING, 49" x 49"
Trudy Søndrol Wasson, Eden Prairie, MN

1201, HAWAIIAN PUNCH, 54" x 54"
Irena Bluhm, Little Elm, TX

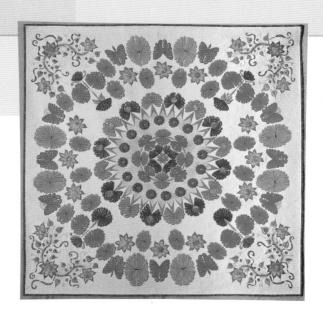

1202, ON THE WEB, 46" x 50"
Mary Jo. Bowers, Chicago, IL

1203, THAT'S AMORÈ, 57" x 53"
Connie Brown & Dort Lee, Asheville, NC

1204, VELVET LEAF, 40" x 42"
Betty Busby, Albuquerque, NM

1205, PLUNKETT'S JUNKET, 50" x 76"
Maureen Squires Capshew, Lanesville, IN

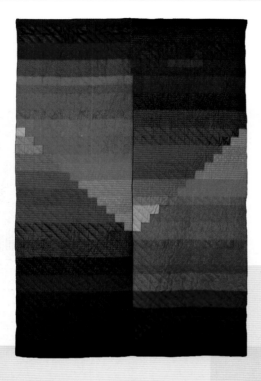

1206, CHAMONIX-ZERMATT, 55" x 78"
Sabine Cibert, Lyon, France

1207, KATRINA CHAOS, 55" x 52½"
Marguerite Lowell Brown Crum
West Lafayette, IN

1208, DIAMOND IN THE SQUARE, 54" x 54"
Ellen Zak Danforth, Fort Collins, CO

1209, GRADING ON THE CURVE, 44" x 49"
Toni Disano, St. Louis, MO

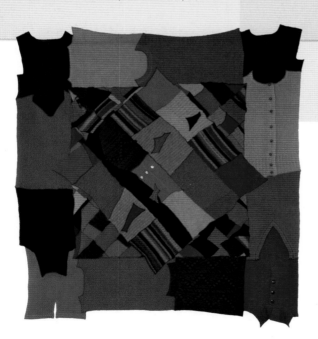

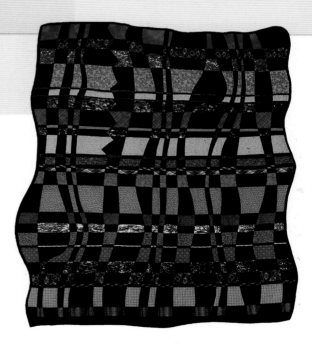

1210, TERROIR – THE ESSENTIAL SENSE OF PLACE
44" x 50½", Barbara Hendrick Dorn, Canton, GA

1211, GRATE, 48" x 48"
Linda Dyken, Mobile, AL

1212, FERN FOREST, 42" x 58"
Karen Eckmeier, Kent, CT

1213, FRUITS AND FLOWERS ENMESHED
40" x 59", Robbi Joy Eklow, Third Lake, IL

1214, ORANGE CONEFLOWERS, 54" x 43½"
Ann Fahl, Racine, WI

1215, SLEEPING DOGS, 60" x 66"
Merry Fitzgerald, D.V.M., Lake Grove, NY

1216, SIX DEGREES OF INTROSPECTION
45" x 66", Laura Fogg, Ukiah, CA

1217, AUTUMN NIGHT, 42" x 84"
Kazuko Funabasama, Ota, Gunma, Japan

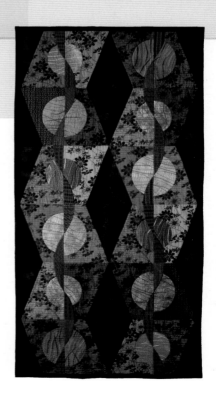

1218, FLORAL FANTASY, 59" x 60¾"
Shirley Gisi, Colorado Springs, CO

1219, LIVING ON THE EDGE, 50½" x 50½"
Sherrie Grob, Murphysboro, IL

1220, UNDULATIONS, 43" x 43½"
Karen Hampton, Evansville, IN

1221, CHILDS PLAY: WISHFUL THINKING
57" x 74", Barbara Oliver Hartman, Flower Mound, TX

1222, THE NUT DOESN'T FALL TOO FAR FROM THE TREE
46" x 43¾", Annette M. Hendricks, Grayslake, IL

1223, ROADS NOT TAKEN, 56" x 56"
Wendy Hill, Sunriver, OR

1224, RED DECO, 60" x 72½"
Jan Hutchison, Sedgwick, KS

1225, THE MASK OF KOREA, 53" x 65"
Mikyung Jang, Seodaemoon, Seoul, South Korea

1226, THE LIGHT SHINES IN THE DARKNESS
40" x 40", Suzanne Kistler, Visalia, CA

1227, WILDFLOWER CONFETTI, 51" x 51"
Kim Klocke, Rochester, MN

1228, GINKGO DANCE, 41" x 40"
Pat Kroth, Verona, WI

1229, TREES, 41" x 49"
Carol MacDougall, Wilmington, MA

Strips 'n Curves: A New Spin on Strip Piecing by Louisa L. Smith. C & T Publishing, Inc.

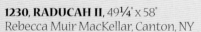

1230, RADUCAH II, 49¼" x 58"
Rebecca Muir MacKellar, Canton, NY

1231, AWAKENING, 40" x 40"
Meta Maclean, TMR Montreal, Quebec, Canada

1232, SURPRISE! 40" x 55"
Suzanne Marshall, Clayton, MO

1233, MORNING DANCE, 56" x 64"
Maggie Marziale, Commercial Point, OH

Inspired by William Frend De Morgan (1839-1917) drawing

1234, MOONLIGHT SONATA, 44" x 48"
Barbara Barrick McKie, Lyme, CT

1235, JUNGLE JUJU, 47" x 47"
Janet Mednick, San Francisco, CA

1236, A QUARTET OF ROSES, 49" x 48"
Hallie H. O'Kelley, Tuscaloosa, AL

1237, WILD CHILD, 40" x 40"
Barbara Olson, Billings, MT

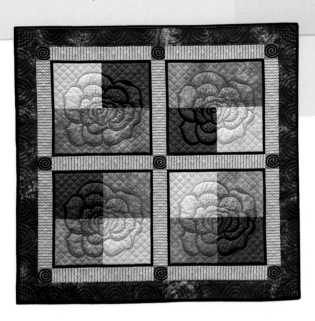

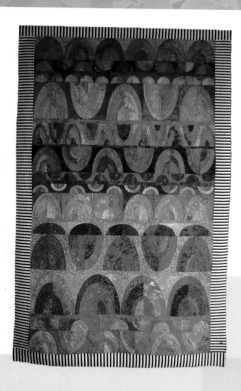

1238, WAVES OF ANGER, 47" x 84½"
Frieda Oxenham, West Linton, Peeblesshire,
United Kingdom

1239, SNOWDROPS IN THE MIDNIGHT GARDEN
44" x 66", Sandra Peterson, Muncie, IN

1240, MICROCOSMIC, 50" x 45"
Jeanne Pfister, Kaukauna, WI

1241, TEA PARTY, 50" x 50"
Liz Piatt, Orinda, CA

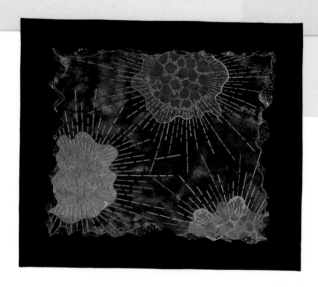

Beauty of the Nile pattern by Claudie Clark Myers

1242, SASSAFRAS SPIRITS, 52" x 52"
Elaine Plogman, Cincinnati, OH

1243, PARTY FAVORS, 44" x 44"
Norma J. Riehm, Hayward, WI

1244, LIGHT BELOW THE SURFACE, 57¾" x 46¾"
Sharon L. Schlotzhauer, Colorado Springs, CO

1245, NEED A LIFESAVER? 46" x 60"
Karen Hull Sienk, Colden, NY

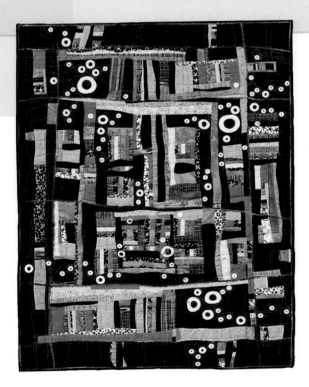

1246, BIG BLOWSY FLOWERS, 49" x 42½"
Sherrie Spangler, Rockford, IL

1248, EMERGING SPRING, 52" x 52"
Rita Steffenson, Urbana, OH

1247, SET ME FREE, 57¼" x 57¼"
Cathy Pilcher Sperry, Cincinnati, OH

1249, RORSCHACH REVISITED, 41" x 49½"
Patsy Thompson, Holland, OH

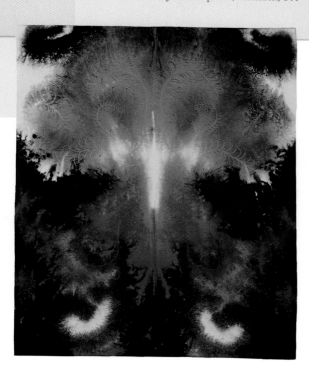

Inspired by Cara Galati's appearance on Simply Quilts

1250, INSANITY, 48" x 48"
Jeanie Sakrison Velarde, Cordova, TN

1251, WOODLAND SIGHTING, 41" x 44"
Cindy Vough, Nicholasville, KY

1252, WOOD NYMPH, 46" x 58"
Yvonne Walter, Canton, OH

1301, SUNDAY MORNING, 59" x 54"
Esterita Austin, Port Jefferson Station, NY

1302, YOU ARE MY SUNSHINE, 51" x 61"
Rosalie Baker, Davenport, IA

1303, THE USUAL SUSPECTS, 45½" x 45"
Nancy S. Brown, Oakland, CA

1304, PAT REACHES QUILTERS NIRVANA
48" x 48", Linda Cantrell, Fletcher, NC

1305, BEYOND THE DIMENSION, 52" x 52"
Eun Ryoung Choi, Seocho, Seoul, South Korea

1306, THE FOREST FLOOR: LUPINE, 42" x 44"
Jean McLaughlin Cowie, Silver City, NM

1307, GORGOSAURUS, 43" x 56"
Amy Cunningham-Waltz, Waltham, MA

1308, FATAL ATTRACTION, 42" x 53"
Sandy Curran, Newport News, VA

1309, OUT OF THE TROPICS: TOUCAN
52" x 66", Grace J. Errea, Laguna Niguel, CA

1310, ONE SUMMER DAY, 58½" x 76½"
Jean M. Evans, Medina, OH

1311, LOOK, LOOK, I SEE IT! 46" x 41½"
Anna Faustino, North Arlington, NJ

1312, ICEBERG FANTASY, 51" x 51"
Laura Fogg, Ukiah, CA

1313, FLORAL VISTA, 44" x 56½"
Cathy Geier, Waukesha, WI

1314, AFRICAN VIGNETTES, 48" x 41"
Lynne Halkett, Pittsford, NY

1315, UNBRIDLED PASSION (SANS FLEUR), 49" x 51"
Denise Tallon Havlan, Plainfield, IL

1316, RED POPPIES, 49" x 60"
Sue Holdaway-Heys, Ann Arbor, MI

1317, FRESH PICKED, 40" x 40"
Ann Horton, Redwood Valley, CA

Workshop by Keiko Goke, Vogue Quilt School

1318, A DAY OF HOPE, 55" x 65"
Donna Hussain, Sacramento, CA

1319, STEP ON A SOFT BREEZE, 41" x 54"
Masumi Kako, Nagano, Japan

1320, JUST THE TWO OF US, 46½" x 44"
Karlyn Bue Lohrenz, Billings, MT

1321, DAHLIA REFLECTIONS #2, 42½" x 42½"
Barbara Barrick McKie, Lyme, CT

1322, COURAGE, 44½" x 45"
Kathy McNeil, Tulalip, WA

1323, TOTEMS, 41" x 56"
Pat Doyle Mikrut, Palos Park, IL

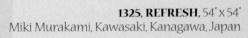

1324, NEW YORK BEAUTY, 51½" x 66"
Mary Kay Mouton, Milledgeville, GA

1325, REFRESH, 54" x 54"
Miki Murakami, Kawasaki, Kanagawa, Japan

1326, SLOWHAND – OLD FRIEND II – YOU GOT THAT RAINBOW FEEL, 53" x 52½", Annedore Neumann, Moenchengladbach, Wickrath, Germany

1327, THE GUARDIANS, 44" x 48"
Nancy Parmelee, Sonoma, CA

1328, EYE OF THE ANCIENTS, 53" x 40"
Andrea Perejda, Arroyo Grande, CA

1329, VINCENT'S SUNFLOWER DAZE, 40" x 52"
Judy Petersen, Pinehurst, NC

Inspired by *Woman with Book by Pablo Picasso*

1330, WATERMELON WINE, 55" x 69¼"
Ruth Powers, Carbondale, KS

1331, LUCY WITH A BOOK, 41" x 54"
Pauline Salzman, Treasure Island, FL

1332, CHIP-N-DALE'S DELIGHT, 40" x 49"
Karen Hull Sienk, Colden, NY

1333, BORN WILD, 41½" x 45"
Gerry Smeltzer, Eureka, CA

1334, DRUMMING UP BUSINESS, 42" x 62"
Marcia Stein, San Francisco, CA

1335, NECTARING, 53" x 74¾"
Nancy Sterett-Martin, Owensboro, KY

1336, VIRTUAL ROSE, 52" x 52"
Mary Tabar, San Diego, CA

1337, MEMORIES OF ROSES, 56" x 55"
Mary Transom, Ohope, New Zealand

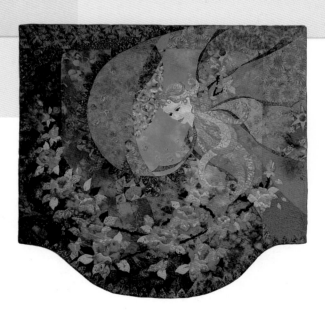

1338, FARM ALARM, 49" x 58½"
Sue Turnquist, Kalamazoo, MI

1339, FRESH SNOW, 41" x 58"'
Elsie Vredenburg, Tustin, MI

1340, PRAIRIE BREEZE, 42" x 48"
Laura Wasilowski, Elgin, IL

1341, BREEZE, 55" x 43½"
Rachel Wetzler, St. Charles, IL

*Borders, Bindings & Edges: The Art of Finishing Your Quilt by Sally Collins, C & T Publishing, Inc.;
workshop by Sally Collins*

1342, SIMPLY FUCHSIA, 44" x 44"
Marlene Brown Woodfield, LaPorte, IN

1401, A DIFFERENT PATH, 43" x 43"
Susan Axelrod, Ramona, CA

1402, RINGS AND PINWHEELS, 54" x 66"
Jenice Belling, Edwardsville, IL

1403, SWAMP ANGEL, 40" x 45"
Caren A. Betlinski, Rushville, NY

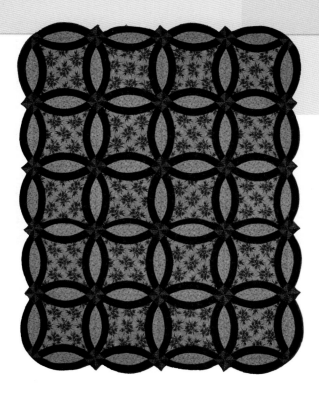

Swamp Angel photo, © Drake Environmental Consultants, E. Bloomfield, NY, used with permission

1404, POKÉMON PALS, 51½" x 64"
Karen Blocher, Unionville, IN

1405, MOUNTAIN SUNFLOWER, 47" x 47"
Annie Buck, Underhill, VT

1406, PLAYING HOOKIE, 45" x 60"
Lisa Calle, Pottstown, PA

1407, WHEN I SEE IRIS, 41" x 47¾"
Deb Cavanaugh, Spring Green, WI

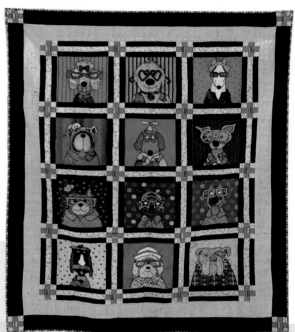

1408, RAJUA, 47" x 56"
Lisa B. Ellis, Fairfax, VA

1409, MUTT SHOTS, 51" x 63"
Margo Z. Ellis, Key West, FL

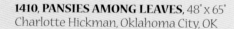

1410, PANSIES AMONG LEAVES, 48" x 65"
Charlotte Hickman, Oklahoma City, OK

1411, SUMMER FLOWERS, 43" x 54"
Bok Young Kim, Paju, Gyeonggi, South Korea

1412, LOS FLORES DE AMIGAS, 58" x 58"
Robin Koehler & Beth Denmon, Troy, IL

1413, CANINE-AMERICANS UNITE! 41" x 53"
Sheila C. Kramer, Rockville, MD

1414, BETWEEN SUNSHINES, 49½" x 49½"
Joung Ae Lee, Kangnam, Seoul, South Korea

1415, SKI VILLAGE, 40" x 51"
Ann Loveless, Frankfort, MI

Cinco de Mayo pattern by Karen K. Stone. The Electric Quilt Company

Jacobean Rhapsodies: Composing with 28 Applique Designs by Patricia Campbell & Mimi Ayars. C & T Publishing, Inc.

1416, JACOBEAN RHAPSODY NO. 5, 48" x 48"
Susan Masulit, Vandalia, MO

1417, ROSES IN MY GARDEN, 53" x 52½"
Helena Mataev, Norwich, NY

1418, REFLECTING ON MY COUNTRY GARDEN
45½" x 45½", Erilyn McMillan, Palmerston North,
New Zealand

1419, WHEELIN N DEALIN, 48" x 48"
Joan Metzger, Sunriver, OR

Simple Blessings: 14 Quilts to Grace Your Home by Kim Diehl. That Patchwork Place; Spring Quintet quilting design by Hari Walner. Mirrorwork workshop by Indra Ahnaimugan.

1420, CHICKEN GIRL, 54" x 47"
Joy F. Palmer, San Jose, CA

1421, WINDOWS TO MY SOUL, 52½" x 59"
Mary Palmer, Innishannon, Co. Cork, Ireland

1422, COLORFUL FUN, 56¾" x 56¾"
Ann T. Pigneri, Louisville, KY

1423, THE BEAUTY OF EMERGING YOUTH
41" x 41", Joyce Ponder, Oxford, OH

Provence Quilts & Cuisine by Marie-Christine Flocard & Cosabeth Parriaud, C & T Publishing, Inc.

1424, SUR LE PONT D'AVIGNON (OVER THE BRIDGE AT AVIGNON),
51½" x 57", Marilyn Smith, Columbia, MO

1425, MEETING WITH THE AUTUMN, 46" x 57"
Kim Joung Soon, Taegu, South Korea

1426, LACE #2, 58" x 58"
Helen Stubbings & Tracey Browning,
Lenah Valley, Tasmania, Australia

1427, DOWN THE GARDEN PATH, 52" x 51"
Dorothy A. Thompson, Port Angeles, WA

Crazy Quilting by Christine Dabbs, Rutledge Hill Press; Painting with Thread by Kit Nicol, Collins and Brown, London, England; and embroidery patterns from Crabapple Hill Designs, and Inspirations Magazine; Issues 11 (1996), 14 & 15 (1997)

1428, CROP CIRCLES, 50" x 62"
Cathy Tomm, Leduc, Alberta, Canada

1429, POT OF GOLD, 59" x 47"
Mary Transom, Ohope, New Zealand

1430, FAUX JACOBEAN TAPESTRY, 59" x 49"
Roxie West, Spring Hill, KS

1431, WYNDLE, 46" x 55"
Lori Winiger, Murray, KY

Jacobean Rhapsodies Composing with 20 Appliqué Designs by Patricia Campbell & Mimi Ayars, C & T Publishing, Inc.

1501, WANDERING FAWNS, 75" x 60"
Rebecca Amendolara, Canby, OR

1502, CLOSE ENCOUNTER, 59" x 59"
Heather Fox, Rainelle, WV

1503, TWILIGHT DANCE, 51" x 64"
Charla Gee, Littleton, CO

1504, SUMMER GARDEN, 47" x 52"
Josie Hermsmeyer, Wildwood, MO

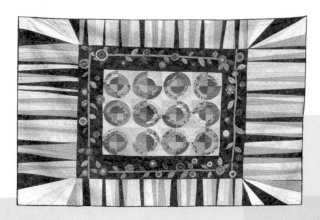

1505, A MIDSUMMER DAY'S DREAM, 80" x 60"
Shannon Burkett Maisel, Allendale, MI

1506, 54–40 OR FLY, 41" x 41"
Kate Flynn Nichols, Billings, MT

1507, PEA – LIME & PAISLEY, 74½" x 92"
Jennifer Shackelford Perdue, Bucyrus, OH

1508, COMPLEMENTARY, 65" x 65"
Gina Perkes, Payson, AZ

Digitized quilting designs by Tanya Del Tongo Armansco, Kay Ott, and Sharon Schamber

1509, RIO GRANDE GORGE-OUS, 51½" x 41½"
Jen Siegrist, Snowflake, AZ

1510, FANTASTICAL DEVIATIONS, 63" x 63"
Susan Webster, Apple Valley, MN

1511, I ASKED THE STARS..., 55" x 55"
Marla Head Whalen, Arlington, TN

1512, HOPE, 75¼" x 89"
Ingrid Whitcher, Pensacola, FL

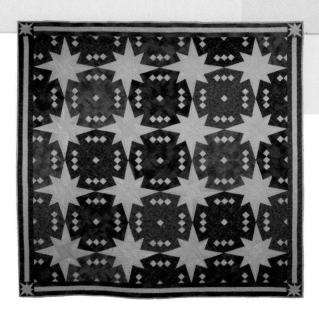

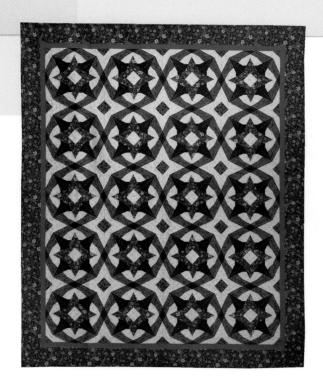

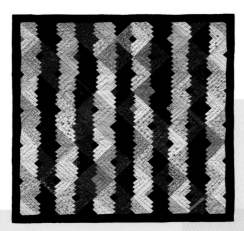

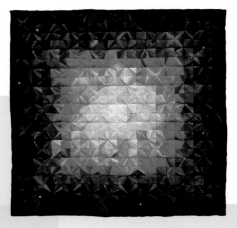

1601, THORNHEDGES, 16½" x 16½"
Connie Ayers, Belfair, WA

1602, GRACE, 12½" x 12½""
Teri Barile, Lorain, OH

1603, NIGHT LIGHTS, 13½" x 13½"
Diane Becka, North Bend, WA

1604, MINIATURE BALTIMORE ALBUM, 17¼" x 17¼"
Rebecca Brown, Glastonbury, CT

Machine Embroidery Makes the Quilt & Creative Projects by Patty Albin, C & T Publishing, Inc.

1605, J'S LITTLE AVIARY, 15½" x 15½"
Betty Carpenter, Belmont, MI

1606, MARY'S HARVEST, 11¼" x 11¼"
Connie Chunn, Webster Groves, MO

Fairmeadow Forget Me Knots: An Album of Appliqué Designs and Nature's Chorus by Jeana Kimball, Foxglove Cottage

Traditional MiniQuilts: 11 Step-by-Step Patterns, Moon Over Mountain Quilters

1607, BABY MONKEYS, 17½" x 17½"
Lee Collins, Columbiaville, MI

1608, TENACIOUS, 23" x 23"
Sally Collins, Walnut Creek, CA

1609, DUTCH HEX, 17" x 17"
Sandy Curran, Newport News, VA

1610, HAWAIIAN DREAMING, 18" x 18"
Judith Day, Lindfield, NSW, Australia

1611, DANCING QUADRILLES, 18" x 18"
Leigh Elking, Scottsdale, AZ

1612, STORM AT SEA, 18½" x 18½"
Sherry Fourez, St. Joseph, IL

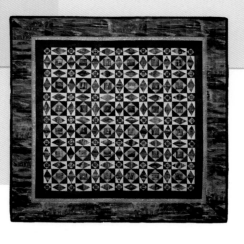

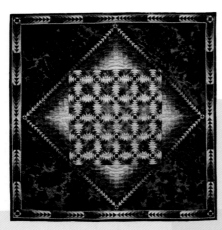

1613, NIGHT CRUISE ON THE RIVER THAMES
20½" x 20½", Kumiko Frydl, Houston, TX

1614, STAGES OF A MARRIAGE, 18" x 17"
Donna L. Gilbert, Fayetteville, PA

1615, TAPESTREE, 14½" x 12½"
Pat Holly, Muskegon, MI

1616, MAD DASH, 20" x 20"
Becky Jackson, Corinth, TX

1617, THE BIRD WITHIN, 16" x 16½"
Susan Jackson, Arroyo Grande, CA

1618, PILGRIMAGE, 6½" x 6.⅝"
Marie Karickhoff, South Lyon, MI

1619, NEW TECHNIQUE, DESPERATELY NEED PUBLISHER
17" x 21½", Mary Kay Mouton, Milledgeville, GA

1621, WITH THE WIND, 19" x 19"
Natsumi Ohara, Yokohama, Kanagawa, Japan

1620, TANGERINE FIREBURST, 18⅝" x 22½"
Judy L. Nelson, Bettendorf, IA

1622, BUTTERMILK BUDS, 12" x 12"
Linda M. Roy, Knoxville, TN

1623, MY FLOWER'S GARDEN III, 18" x 18"
Miyoko Shoda, Kumagaya, Saitama, Japan

1624, SMALL MEDIUM AT LARGE, 7¾" x 7¾"
George Siciliano, Lebanon, PA

1625, DRAMA QUEEN, 16½" x 16½"
Valorie Smith, Enid, OK

1626, CARNIVALÉ, 18" x 18"
Judy Spiers, Foxworth, MS

1627, MIDNIGHT SUN, 11½" x 11½"
Patricia L. Styring, St. Augustine, FL

1628, ANTIQUE BEAR'S PAW VARIATION, 20" x 20"
Loretta C. Sylvester, Palm Coast, FL

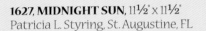

1629, STRAWBERRY BASKETS, 12" x 12"
Alice Tignor, Severna Park, MD

1630, APPLES CROP, 20" x 20"
Mie Totsu, Nagano City, Nagano, Japan

Heaven Scent Miniature 44/2008 by Gay Bomers, Sentimental Stitches

1631, MY FIRST BALTIMORE, 19¼" x 23"
Sharon Ann Waggoner, Springfield, IL

2008 Quilt Contest Rules – Paducah

1. The maker of a quilt can enter a completed quilt by submitting entry blank, entry fee, and images of the completed work.
2. Limit two entries per person, one quilt per category.
3. Quilt must be constructed and quilted by person(s) named on entry blank.
4. Quilts stitched by one or two persons can be entered in all categories except 5. Quilts stitched by three or more people can only be entered in Group Category 5.
5. All quilts must be quilted by hand, by machine, or both.
6. Quilt must have been finished between January 1, 2006, and January 1, 2008, and be in excellent condition.
7. Quilts displayed in any previous AQS Paducah or Nashville contest or made from precut or stamped kits are ineligible.
8. Quilts must be a single unit and not framed with wood, metal, etc.
9. Quilts that combine two or more techniques (other than quilting) should be entered in the Mixed Techniques category (i.e., piecing/appliqué, appliqué/embroidery, piecing/trapunto, etc.)
10. Quilts in categories 4 and 14 must be a first-time entry for any stitchers on the quilt in any Paducah or Nashville AQS contest.
11. Quilt Sizes: (Actual quilt size must fit dimensions listed for category. Quilts longer than 90" must have the rod pocket sewn 90" from the floor for hanging. A quilt label identifying the maker must be stitched to the back lower edge of the quilt.)
    a. Bed-sized quilts in categories 1 – 5 must be 60" to 110" in width and a length of 80" or more.
    b. Handmade quilts in category 6 must be 60" to 110" in width and a length of 80" or more.
    c. Large wall quilts, categories 7 – 10, must be 60" to 110" in width and a length of 40" or more.
    d. Small wall quilts, categories 11 – 14, must be 40" to 60" in width and a length of 40" or more.
    e. Miniature quilts in category 16 must be a maximum of 24" in width and length.

    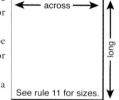

    f. Young Designer quilts in category 15 must be a minimum of 40" or more in width and a length of 40" or more. Quilts can use any traditional or original design elements in a unique interpretation. Young designers must be 18 to 35 years of age (determined on opening date of show).

12. Quilt entries in categories 1–10 will be considered for the Hancock's of Paducah Best of Show, AQS Hand Workmanship, and Bernina Machine Workmanship purchase awards. Quilts in categories 11–14 are eligible for the Moda Best Wall Quilt Award. Quilts in category 16 are eligible for the Benartex Best Miniature purchase award. These purchase awards will become a part of the permanent collection of the Museum of the American Quilter's Society. Winners not wishing to relinquish their quilts may retain possession by refusing their prize money. Photography and printing rights must still be granted to AQS. Quilts in category 15 are eligible for the Olfa Young Designers Okada Award.
13. Quilt must be available for judging and display from April 7 through April 26, 2008.
14. Incomplete, torn, or soiled quilts will not qualify for entry or exhibition.
15. Full-view slide or digital photo must show all edges of the **finished** quilt. Detail slide or digital photo must show the quilting stitches. Please do not send glass slides.
16. All decisions of the jurors and judges are final. AQS reserves the right to reject any entry, including those that fail to follow the quilt contest rules.
17. Please include the complete name and address of your local newspaper so a news release can be sent there.
18. See Categories for descriptions of each category.
19. Semi-finalists may sell their quilts at the show. Additional information will be sent with the acceptance letter.

To enter, send:

(a) Completed and signed entry blank with correct category circled.
(b) Send two digital images with **no modification** including cropping and color correction (one full view of **completed** quilt and one detail of **completed** quilt) on a CD-ROM, using a minimum of 4 MP (megapixel) camera, on **highest resolution setting, saved as a jpeg or tiff file** (be sure to finish the CD and label the disk with your name and title(s) of the work) OR two 35 mm slides (one full view of **completed** quilt and one detail of **completed** quilt). Only one quilt entry per CD-ROM. Photos cannot be e-mailed and CDs and slides will not be returned. Identifying name(s) must not be visible on the quilt in the images.
(c) Entry fee:
AQS members $10.00 per quilt.
Non-members $30.00 per quilt.

Categories

Bed Quilts – width 60" to 110"; length 80" or more
1. Appliqué – predominant technique is appliqué
2. Pieced – predominant technique is piecing
3. Mixed Techniques – two or more predominant techniques, not including quilting
4. 1st Entry in an AQS Quilt Contest – any technique
5. Group – any technique; made by three or more people

Handmade Quilts – width 60" to 110"; length 80" or more
6. Hand – any technique; the entire quilt top must be stitched by hand; backing and binding may be stitched by machine. Long lengthwise seams on the front may be machine stitched.

Large Wall Quilts – width 60" to 110"; length 40" or more
7. Appliqué – predominant technique is appliqué
8. Pieced – predominant technique is piecing
9. Mixed Techniques – two or more predominant techniques, not including quilting
10. Pictorial – representation of a person, place, or thing

Small Wall Quilts – width 40" to 60"; length 40" or more
11. Traditional – uses traditional quiltmaking patterns or designs, including variations
12. Non-traditional – a new creation, not a copy of a previous work
13. Pictorial – representation of a person, place, or thing
14. 1st Entry in an AQS Quilt Contest – any technique

Young Designer Quilts – width 40" or more; length 40" or more
15. Young Designer – any technique in unique interpretation, open to ages 18 to 35 (determined on opening day of show)

Miniature Quilts – width 24" maximum; length 24" maximum
16. Miniature – all aspects of the quilt are in reduced scale

2008 AQS Quilt Contest – Paducah

Entry Blank to Accompany CD-ROM or Slides (this form may be photocopied)

❏ Member $10.00 ❏ Non-member $30.00   Membership #_____/Expiration Date_____

Entrant's or Group Name_____
(Please print)   (This name will be used in the Show Book.)

Street _____ City _____

State _____ Zip _____ Country _____ Postal Code _____

E-mail _____ Phone _____ Fax _____

Complete Name of Newspaper_____ Newspaper E-mail_____

Newspaper Mailing Address _____

Circle One Category Number (see rule 11 for size):

Bed Quilts:
W 60" to 110"; L 80" or more
1. Appliqué
2. Pieced
3. Mixed Techniques
4. 1st Entry– AQS Contest
5. Group – Bed sized

Handmade Quilts:
W 60" to 110"; L 80" or more
6. Hand

Large Wall Quilts:
W 60" to 110"; L 40" or more
7. Appliqué
8. Pieced
9. Mixed Techniques
10. Pictorial

Small Wall Quilts:
W 40" to 60"; L 40" or more
11. Traditional
12. Non-traditional
13. Pictorial
14. 1st Entry – AQS Contest

Young Designer Quilts:
W 40" or more"; L 40" or more
15. Young Designer
Birthdate_____
Miniature
24" maximum, W and L
16. Miniature

Information about your quilt:

Title _____ Size in inches _____ " across x _____ " long

Approx. Insurance Value $ _____ (Over $1,000 requires a written appraisal, maximum value $5,000)

Name(s) of everyone who stitched on this quilt:_____
_____

Brief Description of Quilt for Show Booklet (25 words)_____
_____

Techniques: (Choose all that apply)
❏ Appliqué   ❏ Piecing   ❏ Embroidery   ❏ Trapunto   ❏ Other _____

Quilting: (Choose all that apply)   ❏ Hand   or   ❏ Machine
❏ Domestic (Home) Machine   ❏ Machine Quilting Frame System   ❏ Stitch Regulator   ❏ Shortarm Quilting Machine
❏ Longarm Quilting Machine   ❏ Longarm – Hand Guided   ❏ Computer-Assisted Stitch Software

Design Pattern Source (Choose all that apply: Use separate paper for additional space)
❏ Totally Original (Definition: first, not a copy of a previous work; new creation; patterns by others are **not** used)
❏ Pattern(s) used; list pattern source below

_____ | _____ | _____ | _____
Magazine   Issue   Year   Project Title

_____ | _____ | _____ | _____
Pattern/Book Title   Author   Publisher   Project Title

_____ | _____
Other Artwork title/type   Contact information for artist, publisher, or source

_____ | _____
Workshop title   Workshop instructor

I wish to enter the above item and agree to abide by the quilt contest rules and decisions of the jury and judges. I understand that AQS will take every precaution to protect my quilt exhibited in this show. I realize they cannot be responsible for the acts of nature or others beyond their control. If my quilt is exhibited in the American Quilter's Society Show, I understand that my signature gives AQS the right to use a photo of my quilt for promotion of the AQS Quilt Show in any publications, advertisements, Catalogue of Show Quilts, and other printed or electronic materials. AQS will request permission before using quilts for any other commercial purpose.

_____
signature

Please put your name on the slide mounts or CD-ROM and mail slides or digital images (as outlined in the rules), completed entry blank, and entry fee for each quilt to:

American Quilter's Society,
Dept. Paducah Entry,
PO Box 3290, Paducah, KY 42002-3290

Credit Card (Visa, MasterCard, or Discover)
Card Number ▢▢▢▢ ▢▢▢▢ ▢▢▢▢ ▢▢▢▢   Exp. Date ▢▢▢▢   Ver. Code ▢▢▢   Check # _____

AQS presents the sponsors for the 23rd Annual AQS Quilt Show & Contest. Each category and event is sponsored by a company in the quilting industry. To open the show, company representatives present the cash awards at the Awards Presentation on Tuesday evening.

Best of Show . . . . **Hancock's of Paducah**

Hand Workmanship Award . . . . **American Quilter's Society**

Machine Workmanship Award . . . . **Bernina® of America, Inc.**

Longarm Machine Quilting Award . . . . . **Gammill Quilting Machine Co.**

Best Wall Award . . . . **Moda Fabrics**

Wall Hand Workmanship Award . . . . . . **Coats & Clark**

Wall Machine Workmanship Award . . . . **Brother® International**

Olfa Young Designers Okada Award . . . . . **Olfa® Inc.**

Best Miniature Quilt . . . . **Benartex, Inc.**

Bed Quilts

    Appliqué . . . . **Mountain Mist®**

    Pieced . . . . **Hobbs Bonded Fibers**

    Mixed Techniques . . . . **EZ Quilting® by Wrights®**

    1st Entry in AQS Quilt Contest . . . . . . **Morgan Quality Products**

    Group . . . . **Mettler® Imported by A&E®, Inc.**

Handmade Quilts . . . . **Hoffman California Fabrics**

Large Wall Quilts

    Appliqué . . . . **Fairfield Processing Corp.**

    Pieced . . . . **Baby Lock USA**

    Mixed Techniques . . . . **Robert Kaufman Co., Inc.**

    Pictorial . . . . **C & T Publishing**

Small Wall Quilts

    Traditional . . . . **FreeSpirit/Westminster Fabrics**

    Non-traditional . . . . **Prym Consumer USA**

    Pictorial . . . . **Husqvarna Viking**

    1st Entry in AQS Quilt Contest . . . . . . **YLI® Corporation**

Young Designers . . . . **Olfa® Inc.**

Miniature Quilts . . . . **Benartex, Inc.**

Judges' Recognition . . . . **Possibilities®**

Booth Hop . . . . **Windham Fabrics**

Event Sponsors . . . . **Baby Lock USA, Handi Quilter, Ken's Sewing Center, Outback Steakhouse**

Fashion Show . . . . **AQS, Hobbs Bonded Fibers, Bernina® of America, Inc.**

General Sponsors . . . . **Amazing Designs, American Professional Quilting Systems, Horn of America, Koala Cabinets, PC Quilter, Statler Stitcher™, Superior Threads, TinLizzie 18**

Lecture Series . . . . **Pfaff® Sales & Marketing**

Quilter's Park . . . . **Hinterberg Design**

Teach America 2 Quilt® . . . . **Singer®**

Workshops . . . . **Bernina® of America, Inc., Brother® International, Gammill Quilting Machine Co., Husqvarna Viking, Janome America, Inc., Singer®**

MAQS Workshop Series . . . . **Bernina® of America, Inc., Flynn Quilt Frames, Olfa®, Inc.**

MAQS Rose of Sharon Contest . . . . **Clover Needlecraft, Inc., Fairfield Processing Corporation, Janome America, Inc.**

'07 MAQS School Block Challenge . . . . . . **Moda Fabrics**